THE PASSOVER

Yolanda L. Graham

The Passover
Trilogy Christian Publishers A Wholly Owned Subsidiary of
Trinity Broadcasting Network
2442 Michelle Drive, Tustin, CA 92780
Copyright © 2022 by Yolanda L. Graham
All Scripture quotations are taken from the King James Version of the Bible. Public domain.
No part of this book may be reproduced, stored in a retrieval system, or transmitted by any means without written permission from the author. All rights reserved. Printed in the USA.
Rights Department, 2442 Michelle Drive, Tustin, CA 92780.
Trilogy Christian Publishing/TBN and colophon are trademarks of Trinity Broadcasting Network.
Cover design by: Trilogy
For information about special discounts for bulk purchases, please contact Trilogy Christian Publishing.
Trilogy Disclaimer: The views and content expressed in this book are those of the author and may not necessarily reflect the views and doctrine of Trilogy Christian Publishing or the Trinity Broadcasting Network.
Manufactured in the United States of America
10 9 8 7 6 5 4 3 2 1
Library of Congress Cataloging-in-Publication Data is available.
ISBN: 979-8-88738-121-3
E-ISBN: 979-8-88738-122-0

DEDICATION

I dedicate *The Passover* to my beautiful daughter, Kaniya, who stole my heart the first time I heard her heartbeat. It is because of you that I strive to be the best version of myself every day. You are a true warrior in your own right, and it is an honor to learn from you and to love you. I am so proud of the strong, kind, and determined young lady you have become. Continue to walk in the greatness that God, our Father, revealed to you before you were placed into my womb. Thank you for fighting, and most importantly, thank you for living!

ACKNOWLEDGMENTS

First, I give a special thank you to my Savior, Jesus Christ, for being a lamp unto my feet and a light unto my path (Psalm 119:105). All that I am and all I will ever be is solely because of You. Lord, I truly love You with my whole heart. I pray that I continue to make You proud.

Secondly, I give an enormous, heartfelt thank you to my loving husband and best friend, Kelvin, and our extraordinary children, Kaniya, Kelvin Leon, Kendon Levon, Kaydence, and Destiny (our bonus child), for always having my back, loving me unconditionally, and encouraging me to follow my dreams. My whole purpose in life is to honor and cherish you all until the day I leave this earth. Thank you all for making it so easy to love you.

Additionally, I want to thank two extraordinary women who have made such a profound impact on my life. To my dear sister and friend, Nekishia Cole, thank you for giving me sound advice on developing the book cover. Your heart is so genuine, and you truly are God-sent. Love you. To my mentor, friend, and loving sister, Tracey Anbiya, thank you for showing up during very pivotal times of my life, including during the writing of this book. You have set the example of what it is to be a leader time and time again by giving me much-needed direction as a soldier and as a woman. I appreciate and love you from the bottom of my heart.

Last but not least, I want to thank Katrina Evans-Johnson, Tara Montague, and all the sisters of *Whole Women Matter* for supporting me throughout this journey. The love you all show is so empowering and is a true testament of sisterhood. I love you all.

TABLE OF CONTENTS

Dedication...3

Acknowledgments...............................5

Table of Contents................................7

Prologue...9

Chapter One.....................................13

Chapter Two....................................21

Chapter Three..................................27

Chapter Four...................................33

Chapter Five....................................39

Chapter Six.....................................49

Chapter Seven..................................63

PROLOGUE

It is late in the evening. The sun has gone down—giving the world an indication that it is time for rest. I cruise slowly into the driveway of my home and immediately turn off the engine. Breathing deeply, I remain glued to the seat of my car. My hands grip the steering wheel for dear life as I attempt to prepare myself for the busy household that awaits me. As I remain sitting in my car, I begin to stare at the massive palm tree in my neighbor's front yard. During this cross-examination of the tree, I notice that the structure of the leaves and texture of the bark are unlike the rest of the smaller trees that surround it. I am in total admiration of the palm tree's beauty, uniqueness, and strength.

At this moment, my attention begins to drift toward the current state of my eldest daughter, Kaniya. I begin to reflect upon past experiences of her life, in which I believed that Kaniya was a happy child who was well on her way to conquering the world. It was not until a few years back—two years to be exact—that I discovered that my child was living in a world of darkness, torture, and pain. In my thoughts now, I am flustered and agitated because I cannot, for the life of me, figure out how to

The Passover

help my daughter escape these shackles that have her bound. Time and time again, I pray to God, asking Him to help me see where I am going wrong in taking care of my daughter. In return, I receive no answer; instead, I get defiance, disrespect, and rejection from Kaniya thrown into my face at every given opportunity. Not knowing where to turn, I sit for at least twenty minutes in the car, waiting for that right moment to muster up the courage to step out and face my family. For some unknown reason, I do not want to move. I let out a deep sigh and lie my head against the upper headrest, hoping that peace soon comes to release some of the pressure that has me floored. By God's grace, peace falls upon me. I gather my belongings and head into the house.

Upon entrance, I receive a warm greeting and hug from my younger children, Kelvin, Kendon, and Kaydence. You would think that their gesture of affection would get old, but nevertheless, their kind and genuine embraces warm my heart every time because they act as if I have been gone for decades. Maybe it has to do with the fact that I am always on the go, or perhaps, it is because though I am around them physically, oftentimes, I am not there mentally. I immediately shrug these thoughts away, give my children a hug, and move swiftly to my bedroom. I am anxious for some strange reason, so I take off my uniform, put on something comfortable, and head to my prayer room. My God, all I want to do is just take a few minutes to sit in peace and settle my mind before I prepare dinner.

I turn on the soft, illuminated wall lamps and swiftly crash on the comfortable sitting pillow like a lump of coal. I lie my head against the wall and welcome the warm embrace of total stillness and quietness. At this moment, the Holy Spirit whispers the Book of Exodus into my ear. See, a few weeks before this very day, God drew me to Exodus Chapter 12, which gives knowledge and revelation into the history of the Passover. The Passover is a significant event in humanity's history where God chose to spare the life of every firstborn child whose upper doorpost of their house was covered with the blood of a sacrificial lamb. Reflecting upon Exodus Chapter 12, I ask God, "What am I supposed to be doing?" In this instance, God shows me an image that I will never forget: Kaniya is sitting outside on the ground and holding onto my leg as if her life depends on it. As I look down at her bowed head, she suddenly looks up at me in desperation. Her face is that of a skeleton—it is the facial expression of someone who is dead. Through this warning, the Holy Spirit gives me the direct charge to "fight" for my daughter's soul. He tells me to "wrestle not against flesh and blood, but against principalities, against powers, against the rulers of the darkness of this world, against spiritual wickedness in high places" (Ephesians 6:12). This divine mandate stirs up a fire in me like no other. Forcefully, I begin to speak in my heavenly language as I talk to my Father regarding His business at hand. God directs me to the story of Moses, which depicts how He delivered the children of Israel out of Egypt (Exodus 13) and reveals to me that I must carry this mantle. I receive the instructions that I must repent and cast down every stronghold, break every generational curse, soul tie, and covenant that Kaniya has been subject to since the day she was placed into my womb. God reminds me that in the next seven days, I will be required to pray and fast. God also reminds me that this fast will also take me into the celebration of Pentecost Sunday. God promises me that if I am obedient unto His command and in right alignment with His will, the manifestation of His might will rock my entire household! In His power and in His might, I must suit up in the full armor of God. At this moment, I realize that now is the time for war—it is time to *charge!*

CHAPTER ONE

25 MAY 2020

It is early in the morning. I begin to prepare my mind and spirit for prayer and worship. I feel somewhat tranquil as I settle down in my prayer room and posture my heart for this sacred time with God. During this prayer and worship time, I have an unforgettable encounter with God, my Father. This encounter commences with my wedding day with Jesus Christ, in which God walks me down the aisle to join hands in holy matrimony with my Lord. This encounter is like no other—for my veil is made of diamonds and pearls; my dress is snow white and sculpted to my body like it is my skin. My posture is posed and upright, signifying my authority in the kingdom as a queen who possesses the seal and birthright of Abba, Father. Glory be unto the only true and living God! This encounter sparks the flame of the Holy Spirit

The Passover

within me, and I begin to write my experience in a poem entitled "My Vow." This morning was the first indication of God's promise that He is with me until the end of time and that Jesus, the Christ, is the head of my life—the source of my very existence. I absorb all I can from the Holy Spirit at this very moment and begin to focus on the assignment that my Father has on the agenda for the day. There is no way to brace myself for what the day holds, a day filled with miracles, signs, and wonders—a day filled with the glory of the Lord.

It is now later in the morning. Again, I go into my secret room for another hour of prayer. I am trying to posture my heart in a manner that is pleasing unto God as I lift Kaniya up in the spirit and lay all that concerns her and myself at the altar. During this time, I reflect upon an incident that happened just minutes earlier, in which Kaniya showed a great deal of disrespect. Her demeanor and tone displayed a rebellious spirit that thrived off my frustration and anger. During this prayer time, I seek God's face for guidance as I ask Him to guard my mind, emotions, and tongue. I realize that I, too, am a contributor to the discourse that is running rampant within the four walls of my so-called home. The four walls feel more like a battlefield than a home due to the division and negative influences that have my daughter and me duking it out at any given opportunity. My oh my! God, I ask for peace and rest within my spirit and my home. Now that I am done with prayer, I still feel a sense of defeat. Though I know that the battle at hand is not an easy one, I still feel a sense of disappointment because, again, I am wrapped in my feelings and not trusting the process with my whole heart. Only my God knows the plan that will help me along this assignment. It is His lamp at my feet that guides me and His light unto my path (Psalm 119:105) that allows me to see what is ahead. I shake off the spirit of defeat and doubt to regain my focus. I remember to breathe and hone in on the mission at hand because I cannot fight what I cannot see.

It is now noon, and I am beginning to feel the effects of the fast. My flesh wants food, yet my spirit is hungrier and thirstier for the bread of God. I am determined to hear from my Father on this day because I know deep down that it is the foundation of my will to carry out this mission in accordance with His way. I know that in order for Kaniya and me to see the manifestation of God, I must be obedient and in total alignment with His plan. Therefore, I prepare my mind and heart for afternoon prayer, which is a cooperative prayer with mighty women of God.

The Passover

    This first day of the cooperative prayer opens with us speaking in our heavenly language. Each woman holds distinct authority within the kingdom of God, and it resonates throughout the earthly realm. During this prayer call, my focus is solely on Kaniya and the revelation God gave me concerning her spiritual state. The prayer session is extremely intense right from the start. The weight and glory of God are evident as each woman begins to pray and prophecy is revealed. As my head is bowed, I ask God to give me guidance, courage, and strength to carry the heavy load that is mounted upon my shoulders. I then go into doubt—wondering if I am suited to fight for Kaniya. I wonder whether I have what it takes because I feel like such an immature Christian in comparison to other women within the group. Here I go again, getting entangled with my feelings! As I wrestle with my thoughts, a sudden shift occurs within the room, and one of the anointed women of God begins to speak prophecy over each woman on the prayer call. As the prophetess begins to give me revelation, she declares that I am like a tree planted by the river whose roots run into the water (Jeremiah 17:8) and encourages me to drink. It is then that the very thoughts I wrestled with a moment prior are addressed. God makes it known that I am strong enough to withstand any assignment that He gives me because I am connected to the source, He, God Almighty. I realize that in order to receive and release the full manifestation of His glory, I must drink from the well of Jesus Christ. I must stand firm on the solid rock and push through the race until the very end. At this time, I regain a new level of confidence and begin to refocus yet again on the Pharaoh who stands before me.

Later in the evening, I begin to feast on the living Word by reading Psalm Chapter 1, verses 1–3, and Jeremiah Chapter 17, verses 7–8. I am reminded that I am a blessed being who walks in righteousness—who is in right standing with God. I must continue to study and obey the law of my Heavenly Father and live in a manner that is pleasing unto Him. Like a tree, I am strong; I can withstand the forces of the storm. I am a source of protection; others are enabled to rest under my leaves for shade and comfort. I am created to bear the weight of others; my branches lift them up and enable them to stand upright. I am prosperous; I yield good fruit in and out of season, for my trust and confidence in the Lord, my God, will not allow me to fail. Now, I am filled with more strength as the power of the Holy Spirit falls upon me.

The Passover

In lieu of reading the scriptures, I begin to listen to an Instagram Live video led by Prophetess Tiphani Montgomery. During the live, she makes various focal points from the Book of Acts Chapter 1 regarding the Pentecost. In this chapter, verses 4–5 stand out to me the most for an unknown reason. Here, Jesus provides proof that He is alive and gives instructions to the apostles to not leave Jerusalem but wait for the promise, which is the baptism of the Holy Spirit. As I ponder on this chapter and reflect upon Prophetess Montgomery's lesson, I learn that the Holy Spirit is the gift of Jesus Christ who lives within me. This gift is a part of the trinity, who gives me a direct connection to Jesus and God. Because I am baptized in the Holy Spirit, I have hope or expectations that my Father will enable me to do all things through Christ Jesus, who strengthens me (Philippians 4:13). I now come into the revelation that my hopes are expectations that God will move at any given moment to bestow blessings upon me and all of mankind. I find that delaying or deferring actions to glorify God is an act of disobedience that births stagnation within my soul (mind, emotions, and will). Because of this profound revelation, I realize that there are times when I will be required to plant seeds, and there are other times when I will be required to water seeds. Despite the action I am mandated to take, it is God and only God who makes the increase. Glory to King Jesus!

My time with the Lord suddenly ends, but before I depart my prayer room, I say a prayer to my Father to release the things that concern me in this hour to Him. I ask God to honor my fast for the next seven days in a manner that aligns me spiritually and physically with Him. I ask Him to soften my heart so that I can feel compassion and affection because I know that I lack giving these qualities to both my husband and children. As I begin to utter these words, I feel God's presence and a heaviness covers the entire room like a blanket. With tears in my eyes, I fall on my face and begin to worship and pray to my Father on my knees, which I have not done in an extremely long time. This moment with the Lord is very humbling for me because not only is my body positioned into submission, but my heart is postured into submission as well. This is the beginning of God's will for my life and the undeserving grace that will see us through this treacherous journey. This moment in time enables me to decrease so that the Spirit of God can increase and move forward with wind and fire. I am ready to move forward—I am ready to take all commands from Jehovah Gibbor, my God who is mighty in battle!

CHAPTER TWO

26 MAY 2020

It is early in the morning—around 8:30 a.m., to be exact. I ease out of bed because my youngest daughter, Kaydence, decides to check in at Mommy and Daddy's B&B for the night. I conduct personal hygiene, change into something comfortable, then go into my prayer room to spend some quality time with God. My desire on this day is to have some bonding time with Him, which allows me to have skin-to-skin contact. Like a newborn baby, I can receive all the nurturing needed from my Father that will comfort and sustain me. As I come into His presence, I can literally feel the movement of my cells from head to toe. This feeling is surreal to me at first because it is something new. It is a deeper connection that grants me a more profound revelation into the heart of Abba, Father. As I am infused with Him, I ask to be transformed—to accept my life as a sacrificial offering that will draw mankind unto Him.

In the midst of His presence, I am saturated with His divine power as I feel a deliberate squeeze on my heart. This pressure revives me as if God Himself is performing CPR. His mighty wind is blown back into my body through mouth-to-mouth resuscitation, and the beating of my heart is regulated by the constant compression of His mighty right hand. Peace and clarity stabilize me like a caring nurse who steers me back to health. Praise Jesus for the gift of the Holy Spirit! I begin to speak in tongues, and the Lord suddenly reveals who I am in the spirit. He first shows me that I am a tree. I am strong, supportive, wise, prosperous, and a source of protection, which affirms the prophecy given to me the day prior. Because I asked God a few days before to teach me how to be a wife and mother, the Holy Spirit directs me to read the Book of Proverbs Chapter 31 and outlines in detail the duties I am called to perform. God then shows me again the image of my wedding day, in which I walk down the aisle with Him to join covenant with Jesus Christ. God reiterates that everything I touch will prosper. I am a person of authority who must always walk with my head held high and know, without a shadow of a doubt, that I am a child of El Shaddai, the Almighty God. I receive this revelation with all that I am and begin to stabilize my mind for the unveiling of the remainder of this day. I anticipate that much more will be revealed, and it is an honor to sit at the feet of Jesus.

Now is the time to meet with women of God for cooperative prayer. I go into my prayer room and sit patiently, in a cross-legged posture, on the floor. It is now 12:00 p.m., and all my sisters are in the room suited up. Immediately, we all feel extreme heaviness in the atmosphere. There is a sense of danger in the spiritual realm. I realize at this very moment that we are about to go to war. As we begin to pray in our heavenly language, the intensity of the assignment fills the room. As I press into the fight, I see the yellow eyes of the enemy. These eyes lie in the sockets of a dragon who is ready to devour me with his flame of fire. In this instance, one of the women in the group charges us to fight boldly and fend for ourselves. This is necessary because the enemy is always on standby to attack. God then meets us in the room. His presence is strong and mighty. The Holy Spirit gives us all instructions to guard our eye and ear gates so that the enemy will not gain the upper hand within our family or within us. At the conclusion of the prayer, I am exhausted because the weight of this battle was extremely heavy. I lay all that has transpired in this hour at the feet of my Father because it is not my load to bear. I know that Jesus' yoke is easy, and His burden is light (Matthew 11:30). Therefore, I will continue to move in His perfect stillness—His perfect peace.

There is not a lot going on throughout the remainder of the day. The house is quiet for the most part—no children running around or my name being called from all directions. I feel an overwhelming sense of humility and gratitude as I prepare to shut down for the day. I turn on my YouTube playlist and allow songs to play in no particular order. The first song to greet me is "Way Maker" by Leeland. This song soothes my soul and allows me to let Jesus into the room. In His presence, it is revealed to me that He has made the way, and it is He who is the unleavened bread that I must eat daily to sustain this spiritual journey. This calling upon my life to fight will cause every chain to break within my generational bloodline, causing me and my legacy to be free from the bondage of Satan. The Lord is my shepherd who goes before me and prepares the table before me (Psalm 23). Because He is King, my yes to Him subjects me to His authority alone. I understand that many are called, but few are chosen (Matthew 22:14). As the "chosen," I am willing to fight and intercede for the souls of the lost while simultaneously keeping an eye on my soul to ensure that I am always in alignment with God through Christ Jesus by the Holy Spirit. Wow, I am so grateful for this time. I feel a sense of acceptance and belonging—something I haven't felt in quite a while. No matter how big or small my part is in my Father's plan here on earth, I am honored that He chose *me* to be a part of His royal family!

CHAPTER THREE

27 MAY 2020

It is 3:00 a.m. I lie in bed, half awake, trying to get myself focused and ready for prayer. I finally push myself up; the battle with slothfulness tries to challenge me. Not today! I will not give into the enemy and allow procrastination to steal the opportunity of me entering my Father's presence. I conduct personal hygiene and enter the war room with a refreshing feeling that propels me to get ready for battle. I begin to recite the iniquity and fasting prayer that was given to me by Prophetess Katrina Evans-Johnson. As I meditate upon the words, I begin to go into warfare by speaking in tongues. As I speak in tongues, the Holy Spirit informs me that I am waring on behalf of my own soul and my entire family. Thankful for the Holy Spirit, God's presence is evident yet again. God reveals to me that all assignments of the enemy have been aborted, and the battle (at this present time) has been defeated. I rest in the comfort of my Father's love as I close my eyes and take in His *Ruach*—the very breath of the Spirit of God.

As I am released, I make my way back to bed, for this waring has depleted me for some unknown reason. I lie in bed, staring at the ceiling with the aim of finding sleep. It does not come. Instead, God places my thoughts on my relationship with my husband and children, and I begin to reflect upon my interactions with them. I realize that there is a great distance between us. This gap has been strongly present since my redeployment from Afghanistan in 2013. Seven years later and the effects of my experience in that foreign land still have a strong grip on the well-being of my life and home.

I begin to talk to Jesus and ask Him to grant me peace, and with this gift, I also ask Him to clothe me in the spirit of affection so that my family may witness and feel His heart and love. My despise of the anger I carry taps me on the shoulder, and I ask my Lord to free me from this bondage—to transform me in such a way that this sin becomes powerless within my soul. My plea is surely heard because God lays peace and rest upon me like a tailored dress that fits every curve of my body.

In this instance, I feel the heaviness of the glory of the Lord, and I fall into a deep sleep that lasts for hours.

I wake up to the brightness of the sun. I check the time and discover that it is 9:00 a.m. I notice that I feel a refreshing; wow, that deep sleep was necessary! I have the desire to check my Facebook page, but the Holy Spirit shakes His head and instructs me to do otherwise. I am not sure of the exact plans for the day, so I lie in the bed a few minutes longer. There are no thoughts dancing in my mind and no motivation to move at this very second, just the desire to lie still with no cares of the world. This peaceful experience is short-lived as the beeping of my phone alerts me that a post on Facebook has surfaced. With the Holy Spirit's permission, I check my page and find that Prophetess Katrina is speaking on a live video in *Whole Women Matter*. The intensity and energy in her voice echo throughout my room as I listen to her teaching on the presence of the Holy Spirit and the effect of cycles. This subject strikes a great interest within me. Lord knows that in many areas of my life, I am like a hamster in a cage, running on a ridged wheel. For today, I have decided to keen in on the cycle of anger and rejection. Prophetess Katrina points out the meaning of a cycle and notes that it is an act of doing something over and over again. In regard to life, she shares the notion that doing something repeatedly with the desire to achieve a different result is insanity at its finest. Nodding my head convincedly, I realize that in order to see change, I must do something that I have never done before. I must cast my net on the other side of the boat to witness the promise and miracle of God. As prayer begins, I ask for deliverance from the yoke of anger. I feel a sense of hope and determination to keep pushing and to keep my eyes on the prize. For surely both Kaniya's and my soul are on the line. By God's grace and the help of Jesus Christ, it is guaranteed that the enemy will not win. Five days remain until the celebration of Pentecost. I am not sure what God is about to do. But whatever it is, I know that it is going to be *big*!

Later in the evening, I lie in bed with the intention of spending more time with the Lord. My door opens abruptly, and I look up, expecting Kaydence to come in. No, it is not Kaydence, but it is Kaniya. She does not say anything, and immediately, she rushes over to the bed and lies next to me with a light hug. I can feel the tension resonating from her small body. Maybe it is because we do not engage in affectionate interactions often, or maybe it is because I, too, feel tense, and the energy is bouncing off of me. Suddenly, Kaydence enters the room, jumps on the bed, and hugs me from behind.

I let down my guard and embrace this moment—a gift of loving upon two of the most important people in my life. For the first time in ages, I genuinely feel warmth and love in my heart. This connection makes me realize that, like Kaydence, Kaniya will always be a baby to me. She will always need attention, nurturing, motivation, and cultivation. As her mother, I vow to be who God has charged me to be. It is my responsibility to fulfill my obligations inherited in being the nucleus of this family. With all that is within me, I will continue to fight, and so help me, God, I will be victorious!

CHAPTER FOUR

28 MAY 2020

I am excited this morning. Normally, I am lagging and dragging because, to be honest, it takes me a minute to warm up, get my mind together and move. 9:00 a.m. is approaching fast, and it comes to my mind that God did not awake me as early as He had done in the past days. Maybe He saw it fitting for me to rest longer because He surely knows what this day holds, or perhaps, being the gracious God that He is, He simply just decided to let me be. No matter the reason, I am thankful for the much-needed and peaceful sleep. Taking a deep breath, I sit up, stretch my arms, and get dressed for work. Driving to work is quiet today. My thoughts regarding family, work, rest, and the future are ebbing and flowing, which gives me the desire to release the concerns of my heart to God. I drive into the parking lot at my job and decide to sit in my car until nine. It is close to time for cooperative prayer with the women in *Whole Women Matter*, so I log into the group and wait patiently for the opportunity to let go of all that troubles me today. During this day of fasting and iniquity prayer, I carry the heaviness of repentance like an eighty-pound rucksack on my back. I flashback to the previous day, in which I was not totally consecrated to God. To be completely transparent, I know the television was my idol on this day, which explains the reason why I found it extremely difficult to stay on track and fully commit to my scheduled alone time with the Lord. Disappointment looks down on me, and I feel a sense of remorse. Humbly, I ask God to forgive me for allowing the television to be my god and inviting distraction to move in like an inconsiderate roommate. Suddenly, I feel His presence and glory. Immediately, I am forgiven—my slate is washed clean! Feeling liberated, I see that the prayer call has ended. I adjust my mind to focus mode so that I can tackle the issues of the soldiers within my company. I am certain that the situations awaiting me will not let me down when it comes to being remarkably mind-blowing, to say the least. With a light sigh, I make my way into the workplace. With meetings, appointments, and First Sergeant duties thrusting me throughout the day, my hectic season comes to an end.

Sitting at my desk, I pinch the bridge of my nose and try to regroup from all that has transpired today. God feels my distress and allows peace to welcome me with open arms. Gratefully accepting, I hug peace for dear life. I make the choice to leave all that has happened during work hours at work and prepare myself for my family, who awaits me at home.

An hour later, I am finally home. Making a detour to the grocery store seems to have taken the little bit of energy that I had left. I know that I must go inside and get dinner ready. It is already after 6:00 p.m., which pushes me to meet my goal of having dinner prepared by 7:00 p.m. Gripping the door handle, I am not sure of what to expect exactly. All I know is that I feel something good because God has been revealing subtle, positive changes within the entire family and me. As I enter the house, I notice that everyone is upstairs. Though this may seem small, I am grateful because I am afforded the opportunity to change out of uniform in peace. Dropping the groceries on the counter, I shuffle to the bedroom with my uniform jacket already in hand. I bombard the bedroom and sit on my bed to take off my boots. Ah, this simple action never gets old because it brings great pleasure to drop that load from my feet every single time. Sitting in silence, I wonder how the children's day went with school and all. Things are definitely unusual, being that COVID-19 has thrown a grenade, shattering any sense of normalcy in their lives. Nevertheless, I rest assured in the promise that God has them in His hands, and like all weapons formed against them, it too will not prosper—they shall overcome.

I sit my current thoughts to the side and throw on some sweats. I make my way to the kitchen and begin cooking dinner. With music playing, I am consumed by the richness of the words that praise Jesus Christ. I am at peace at this very moment, and on many levels, I feel a sense of calmness. I hear the trampling of footsteps on the stairwell and immediately recognize that the pitter-patter of little feet is Kaniya's. She enters the kitchen with that cat-like grind that I love so very much. I return the smile and notice that Kaniya has a lightness about her today. I am taken by surprise because I have not seen this glow on her for such a long time. The joy that clothes her at this present moment is what I pray covers her every day of her life henceforth. It is a gift that can only be given by Christ Jesus, who is the lamp unto her feet and the light unto her path. May He lead her beside still waters and restore her soul (Psalm 23:3)! Kaniya and I have a light conversation about her day. It seems as if she wants to talk a great deal but decides to give me details in small chunks. I am certain that her reluctance to speak freely and deeply has a lot to do with my quick dismissals or, perhaps, the fact that I am always so occupied with my career. There it is! I am faced with the truth that I place all my energy into those in the Army, leaving her the scraps. At this moment, this revelation hits me like a bulldozer, which knocks the wind out of me. It takes me a minute to regroup, but I do so with my head held low. This conviction chisels at the stone of my heart, and I immediately go into repentance, asking God to forgive me. As Kaniya continues to talk, I notice that she is a compassionate child who just wants to be heard and understood. I, too, know what it feels like to want others to legitimately hear me and appreciate my thoughts and actions. Standing in front of Kaniya, I feel such shame because I am a hypocrite who is currently experiencing this very thing in my adulthood. My God, I now realize that I bury this feeling every day by trying to save everyone else, which explains why I always have the urge to jump in to defend or save those in my workplace! It seems as if Kaniya feels my sadness. She opens her arms and says, "Mom, I just want a hug." Embracing her tightly, I feel my heaviness lifted. My oh my, this brave girl has no idea how much her hug comforts me in this hour. Truth be told, God knows that I needed this connection more than she did. Father, thank You because Your goodness and mercy endure forever. Amen.

CHAPTER FIVE

29 MAY 2020

This morning was quite different. It appears as if my mood is much lighter because the heaviness of my many burdens has been lifted. Praise be to God! The song "Way Maker" by Leeland has been echoing in my mind for days now, and I cannot shake the feeling that my spirit is placed under a magnifying glass. At this very moment, I can feel God's eyes keening in on me as His powerful light pierces my heart and mind. His light begins to spark a fire within me, removing the residue of all my iniquities, which is surely cleansing me literally from the inside out. Jesus, praises to You, my King, for my deliverance! As I lie on my side, I take a glance into the bathroom and notice that Kelvin is standing at his sink, brushing his teeth in preparation for work. I just lie there to watch him for a second, thinking of all the things we

The Passover

have endured so far on our journey as husband and wife. My God, it has been twenty-three years already, and I know that this ride is not slowing down anytime soon. I find comfort, though, in knowing that God created my husband specifically for me. His character, his morals, and his place in God are like no one I have ever seen. I am so fascinated by his very existence, but more often than not, I fail to show that I honor and appreciate him. Once again, at this very moment, I am convicted. I pray silently in repentance for submitting to my own selfishness and wasteful ways. I acknowledge that my ungratefulness not only affects our children (in ways I cannot possibly imagine) but also tears down the very substance within Kelvin's soul that makes him a mighty man of God. I ask my Father to reconcile us as a family and make this house a home filled with compassion, forgiveness, unity, and love. As Kelvin begins to walk out of the bathroom, I spring abruptly out of bed. We begin to have a long, drawn-out conversation regarding our agenda for the day. Suddenly, I feel a light shake from the Holy Spirit. He points out to me that I am responding to my husband in an irritable manner for no reason at all. Hold up! I know that I am a bit hungry due to fasting, but the agitation is not coming from that. Immediately, I revert to the heart-to-heart conversation I just had literally minutes ago with God. In this instance, Father reveals the scheme of the enemy and all the smoke he brings along with him. Sheesh, he wastes no time! Fed up with his presence, I step on Satan's neck and tell him to stand down because he will not have any authority in this house today. I immediately take action by going into prayer—handcuffing him and his demons (and all their mess) and escorting them all back to hell where they belong. See, to flee from Satan, I must first recognize that the stranger is present. Now that my work at this present time is done in the spirit, the feeling of agitation immediately disappears. Now, Kelvin and I can finish our conversation with decency and order. For the first time in a while, my husband does not leave the house with frustration riding his back like an annoying monkey who refuses to get down. I pray that his day is light and blessed.

The children are making their way downstairs to eat breakfast before school starts. I am staying focused because I have a lot on my agenda to complete today. It is day five of the fast, and I notice that my lack of tolerance for abstaining from food has decreased, but my hunger for the presence and Word of God has increased. All I crave in this disposition of time is His company, the concerns of His heart, His knowledge, and most importantly, His love. As I come out of my most inner thoughts, I notice that the children are settled in place, ready to begin class. I am so proud of their willingness to follow instructions and move in the spirit of obedience. The opening of class has now begun, so I am able to tidy up the house and check in on Kaydence to ensure that she is settled as well. Today is off to a great start. My intention is to complete the task set for the house and then step out to run errands as soon as the children's school day is over. It is now later in the afternoon. I am dressed and ready to head out into town. Before I walk out of the door, I briefly speak with Kaniya and give her instructions on coverage of her brothers and sister until I return. She takes a mental note and goes upstairs to close out her school session for the day. Stepping outside, I notice that the weather is pleasant. To be completely honest, the temperature, the blueness in the sky, and the noticeable calmness in the atmosphere are truly breathtaking! I appreciate this day because it is one that I have never seen before, and once it is over, I will never see it again. Thank You, Father, for this day—this present I am given by You to unwrap. The unveiling reveals Your purpose in the very hours, minutes, and seconds, which moves like a steady beat that constantly sounds by the command of You, the Almighty.

Driving down the busy highway, I can feel God finalizing something. I am not sure what it is at the moment, but I am certain that God is aligning things concerning my house (family) in their proper place. In the comfort of this revelation, I turn on my worship playlist, and I begin to worship by listening to the songs "I Will Exalt You" by Musiq City and "Withholding Nothing" by William McDowell. During this hour, God reveals how majestic He is, and in return, I feel such an honor that I am allowed into His presence. Absorbed in my Father's glory, I feel a warmth, and then suddenly, a light blow of air fills the car. God reveals to me that He backs me up and will continue to back me up every time! It is such a humbling feeling to know that my Lord and all of heaven have me covered. His protection and His love are like no other. Yahweh, You are the I AM. I submit to You and to You alone. May Your plan for my life and my generations to come be carried out in a manner that honors and glorifies You! *Shalom.*

It is late in the evening. Dinner is done, the children have eaten, and I am awaiting Kelvin to come home from work. God, this man works diligently to provide for his family. I pray that You bless him from the crown of his head to the soles of his feet. Let all that he thinks, all that he says, and all that he does be a living testament to how

The Passover

great You are! I am filled with love for this man, and I pray that I cherish him in all that I do. As I sit in my thoughts, Kaniya enters my room. She has this frustrated look in her eyes that alarms me that she has something gigantic on her mind. She looks at me hesitantly at first; then, something shifts her thought pattern as if she received the green light that I am a safe place. She expresses to me that she has great concern about how she pours into others (her family, friends, etc.) and does not get the same pouring in return. She gives me a vivid description of the dream she had the night before, in which her hair fell out. I am aware that I do not possess the gift to interpret dreams, but the Holy Spirit gives me the unction to Google "hair fall out interpretations." The Google search results show us that hair loss can be symbolic of feeling helplessness or fear of a situation in your life that causes you to feel powerless. As we embark upon this new revelation, I encourage Kaniya to express how she feels at this very moment. She tells me that oftentimes, those she considers close to her speak down and are negative to her to make her feel small. She acknowledges that she has always felt peculiar (as the odd ball), in which her views of things never line up with those she associates with, resulting in her feeling a sense of loneliness. As she speaks, the very reflection of me flashes before my eyes. Kaniya is literally walking in my shoes! My heart tugs and the motherly instinct in me flares up because, at this moment, I only want to protect my cub. I know that in order to do so, I must speak life into her because the power lies within my tongue. I tell her that she is created to be set apart because her spiritual gifts will shine in all that her hands touch. I tell her that she is a child of God, and because of this, she is a queen who bows her head to no one but the Father. I feel the Spirit of God in the room, and I begin to plant the seeds of her future (power, love, a sound mind, freedom, good health, strength, and prosperity), which will begin to blossom from this day forth. I tell Kaniya that I relate to her on so many levels because being peculiar, isolated, and giving is part of our godly DNA that must be protected at all costs. The oil over her life is sacred and must be treated as such! I let Kaniya know that I am her friend, her sister in Christ, and her mom, who will always be available until the day God calls me home. She gives me the cat-like grin that she is infamous for and expresses that though it may not seem like it sometimes, she not only loves me, but she truly likes me! To hear her say these words brings tears to my eyes. We enjoy each other's company for hours. In her fifteen years of life, we have never spent this much time together in one setting alone. At this moment, I realize that Kaniya has never really experienced closeness with family and friends because she has been shifted around like a wanderer all of her life due to my obligations to the military. Because of my assignments in the military, it is my responsibility to be her close companion. It is now that amends are birthed, and our rightful relationship begins. She kisses me on the cheek and thanks me for being a listening ear. She departs the room with a lightness about her, which fills me with overwhelming joy. God now shows me that when Kaniya takes her thoughts and releases them out of her mouth, she is freed from the attacks of the enemy. I now know that it is my duty to be accessible to her because the more I am free in the spirit, the lighter her burden will become. I praise You, Father, for Kaniya's existence. Thank You for Your grace, mercy, and sudden move in both of our lives. May You continue to remove the scales from her eyes so that she can see clearly in the spirit; open her ears so that she can hear You and know when it is Your voice speaking; reveal Your secrets to her in the many dreams to come. Amen.

As I prepare for bed, I am compelled to go into my secret place for prayer. I politely go into the room because I know Father wants me to reflect upon today. As I take my seat and prepare the atmosphere to welcome God, the Holy Spirit directs me to go to my worship playlist on YouTube to listen to "Prophetic Intercession (Live in ATL GA) Featuring Prophetess Sharde Martin." I press play and allow this powerful intercession to take root in my spirit. As I am feeding off of the Word of God, I hear Him say, "Rebirth." God shows me that a revival—an awakening—is stirring within the spirit and soul of both Kaniya and me. The dry, desolate places are now being nurtured by the living water, Jesus Christ. I bow to the Almighty in this revelation, and nothing but total submission is my portion. I continue to worship, and the song "Psalm 23 (I Am Not Alone)" by People and Songs Featuring Josh Sherman begins to play softly in the background. The warmth of God's presence comforts me, and then suddenly, the vision of the day of Kaniya's middle school formal dance flashes before my eyes. On this beautiful day, Kaniya is sitting in her formal gown, staring out of the window. As she looks out the window, she lifts her eyes unto the hill from which comes her help. Her help comes from the Lord, who made heaven and earth (Psalm 121). This image is a sight to behold. Her posture, her demeanor, and her expression radiate that of power, royalty, and birthrights. Father assures me again that Kaniya is not alone. I give Him praise as tears roll down my eyes. He instructs me to send the song to her phone via text and allow it to minister to her spirit. I do as I am instructed and allow Great Jehovah to do what only He can do—*be God!*

CHAPTER SIX

30 MAY 2020

It is around 5:50 a.m. I wake up with thanksgiving in my heart and praise upon my lips. This is another day in which I have no urgency to move right away, so I continue to lie in bed and reflect upon the prayer and worship that transpired last night before bed. I am again filled with love for God because His grace and mercy are everlasting. As I continue to parlay like I just received a deep tissue massage, my mind shifts to last night's battle with temptation around 11:30 p.m. Right before the midnight hour, my flesh decides that it wants to rise against me. I am extremely hungry, not just a little stomach grumbling that can be satisfied with a glass of water, but a legit, no desire to eat something—anything! In this moment, my spirit realizes that the enemy knows that I am close to a breakthrough not only for my daughter but myself and will use any tactic available to throw me off course. Not tonight, Satan; get ye behind me in the mighty name of Jesus! My time with God through prayer, worship, and the studying (eating) of the Word of God is far more important than food. It is an honor to partake in such an experience—to make this sacrifice (the offering of my flesh) for the sake of my purpose and the prosperity of my generations to come. Therefore, to combat my flesh, I begin to sing a short interlude by CeCe Winans. I ask Him to feed me the living bread that will fill me up and make me whole. After singing this song over and over, the hunger begins to subside, and God places me into a deep sleep. Wow! Father, You are so attentive and caring! I am now pulled back to the present. Shaking my head in total humility, I thank God again for the changes He has brought forth in both Kaniya's and my life. I now have the motivation to move, so I get up to get dressed for the day.

It is later in the morning. I have completed my errands, and I am now driving down the quiet highway headed back home. During this drive, there is no noise—only the rumbling of the engine and my thoughts dancing around in my head like ballerinas gracefully sashaying across a gigantic stage. I commence praying to Father, thanking Him for all that He has done for us so far in this experience. Before I go any further in prayer, the words "transform tomorrow" flash across a nearby billboard in vibrant colors. This sign fills me from the inside out because it seems as if God is speaking to me in this hour—giving me foresight that He is about to make a mighty move on this upcoming Sunday, in which we will commemorate the day of Pentecost. As the song "I Am Not Alone" repeatedly plays in my mind, my heart leaps for joy, and I smile and praise my Lord even more for never leaving us or forsaking us.

I finally make it home. It is Saturday, so the house should remain quiet for quite some time because the children stayed up a bit late last night. I seize to take advantage of this time and head to my prayer room to spend some extra time with God. While sitting in Father's presence, I am ushered by the Holy Spirit to Google the significance of Mount Sinai because of Kaniya's middle name, "Lasha," which Kelvin and I chose from the Bible before she was born. Examining the search results, I find that Mount Sinai is considered one of the most sacred locations in the Jewish, Christian, and Islamic religions. It is here that God gave Moses His law, the Ten Commandments. This finding is extremely profound to me, so immediately, I refer to the meaning of Kaniya's middle name, Lasha—which means "a place

The Passover

east of the Dead Sea (Genesis 10:19) that marks the limit of the country of the Canaanites"—and analyze its correlation to Mount Sinai. This research gives me the revelation that Kaniya is sacred and possesses the authority to *touch nations*! This explains why Satan is so determined to steal her calling (identity), kill her purpose, and destroy her lineage to come. No, no, no... this will not come to pass on my watch! I begin to pray and worship the Lord with my whole heart, believing that all things will work together for our good because we love Him and are called accordingly to His purpose (Romans 8:28).

My prayer and worship to the Lord continue to flow like a calming and gentle stream. As I continue to abide in God and He in me, He gives me the image of a purple lotus and tells me that I am this. My name, Yolanda, means a "violet flower." This is so beautiful to me because now, Father has given more distinction to my identity in Him and the purpose of my life. See, the purple lotus is a unique flower because it grows in the southern swamps of Stygia and is not commonly found. This flower closes and falls to the water at night and rises back above the water at daybreak (its life cycle). The purple lotus has this uncanny ability to plunge into murky water (mud) and come back to life unscathed.

This brave flower defies logic and is fascinating due to its will to *live*! It resurrects itself over and over again, returning just as beautiful as it was last seen. This flower exemplifies unwavering faith and carries the attributes of ascension, enlightenment, and rebirth. As the tears flow down my cheeks, I feel a sense of love and empowerment. Immediately, I lift my head, and, as clear as a noncloudy day, I hear God say, "Go now, and impart your new mantle into your daughter, for the more you operate in this authority, so shall she." I take the instructions of the King and begin to pray once more on behalf of my beloved daughter.

It is almost noon, and I have the urge to visit my Father in our secret place while the kids enjoy themselves at home. They are calm on this fine Saturday, and I am grateful that the spirit of peace rests upon them today. Sitting in my prayer room, I check the time once more because I will link up with women of God to participate in noon prayer. It is fifteen minutes to 12:00 p.m., so I reach for my phone to play my beloved musical list. The desire to worship and praise God hits me, so immediately, I tap "Blessings on Blessing" by Anthony Brown and Group Therapy. Bobbing my head and waving my hand like David, I praise the Lord with all that I have. Yes, the Spirit of the Most High always shows up! Taking advantage of being in His presence, I continue to praise Him. Still in my vibe, I log into Zoom to join the prayer group. As the women enter the room, you can feel the energy of power and victory. We all begin to praise and worship God by chanting and cheering for the coming of the Holy Spirit. We begin to sing, "We ready, we ready." The Holy Spirit enters the room like the guest of honor and graces us with the anointing of God. We continue to worship in spirit and in truth and ask Him to open our hearts to be suitable, reachable, obtainable, prepared, and conditioned to hold the weight of the Lord. God reveals to us in this very hour that we will thirst no more because He has made provision in the wilderness. The living water springs from us from the feet up! During this exciting experience, I can literally taste the sweetness of milk and honey, which burns my throat. Outside, I notice that the birds are chirping—they, too, are in alignment with God Almighty. Suddenly, I hear God say that He is proud of me today! I have no words. Only the manifestation of uncontrollable tears flowing down my face can express the gratitude I feel as I lie in the welcoming arms of my Father. The prayer session is now coming to an end, but before we are released, a prophet of God speaks and gives us instructions to make a declaration before the Lord. Without hesitation,

I declare and decree that the Holy Spirit is now erected in my life. My top is off. In the name of Jesus, my vessel is not hidden but on display. I am now the river of God's living water. I am the ripple that causes things to move and causes ships to wreck. Because of my anointing and authority in Christ Jesus, I *war*! Everything that God has given me in spirit will now collide with my natural (reality)! I am the collision course, and it is necessary for those called and assigned to me! Glory to Lord Jesus, who is a lamp unto my feet and a light onto my path (Psalm 119:105)! As the heaviness sits on my chest like a sleeping elephant, I realize that God has graced me for this hour. I appreciate the act of fasting because it opens the portal for God to move with more intense force! Moving forward, I now know that in life, God uses me to plant and water the seed, but it is *He* who makes the increase. Glory to the great Jehovah!

Wow! This prayer experience has me in a tranquil state. I can still feel the glory of the Lord, so I continue to praise and worship. "Alexa, turn on gospel music," I command. Immediately, "Love Theory" by Kirk Franklin begins to blast from the tiny speaker. As I prepare brunch for the kids, I dance around the kitchen like no one is watching. Each time I release the words of the song from my mouth, it tugs at my heart like a rope being pulled by

The Passover

a great force that accelerates my soul. I rejoice because these words touch me differently today. Just moments before, in prayer, my Father literally said that He was proud of me, so to hear the words during this time, in this hour, gives me so much life! I take advantage of this recharge and commence making final preparations for the meal. The song comes to an end, and the song "Here Again" by Elevation Worship fills the room. I cannot explain the feeling I am experiencing right now, but I am completely overtaken by a peaceful presence that has caused every cell, nerve, and sense within my body to yield. As the words to the song penetrate my heart, I begin to go into a trance. All I can literally do is sway side to side. With my head lifted and eyes closed, I welcome Jesus into my space. I must be in this state for quite a while because suddenly, I open my eyes and realize that the music is no longer playing. I stand still to gain my composure, and as I do so, I hear the Lord say, "Yes, I will meet you." I smile and begin to give Alexa the order to play more music. Urgently, the Holy Spirit says, "No, leave it off and enjoy My stillness—My peace." In total obedience, I move in silence. As I do so, the Holy Spirit reveals to me that on 31 May, I must gather with Kaniya in prayer and worship. During this time, Kaniya and I must come out of covenant with all wicked spirits (depression, suicide, darkness, anxiety, insecurity, low self-esteem, rejection, invalidation, instability, deception, manipulation, desolation, displacement, orphanage, isolation, abandonment, offense, defense, doubt, fear, loneliness, resentment, uncertainty, and turmoil) that gained access to her in the womb because they resided in me. Once all evil spirits have vacated, the empty spaces must be filled with the fruit of the Spirit, which is love, joy, peace, longsuffering, kindness, goodness, faithfulness, gentleness, and self-control (Galatians 5:22–23). Accepting the instructions, I set my mind in motion regarding the new revelation God has given me. I am so confident because my Father has allowed me to enter the secret place in which He gives me the concerns of His heart. My oh my, I am so honored! I walk over to the dinner table with a small serving of the meal I have prepared because the fasting period is over for the day. I try to eat, but my stomach is so full of the Spirit of God. I can only eat tiny bites as if my stomach is the size of the singing birds I heard earlier. This experience brought forth the confirmation that I am now in total alignment with God and His will for my life and Kaniya's life. I am grateful for Jesus' faithfulness and His constant devotion to the well-being and restoration of our souls. Hail, hail to the Lion of

The Passover

Judah!

The remainder of the day carries a light essence. Kaniya comes downstairs with a refreshing look on her face and greets me. She tells me that she feels freer today and that she wants to tell me about the dream she had last night. I am bracing myself because, as of lately, she has only been having horrid dreams. Kaniya begins recalling the dream and states that she received all As in her course of study. She says with astonishment that she was wearing a white coat as if she were a doctor of some sort. See, Kaniya has the aspiration to become a veterinarian. As she continues to tell me the remainder of the dream, I hear God say that she has the gift to dream and prophesy. I smile in return of this revelation and share with Kaniya what God told me and what having the gift to dream and prophesy means. She soaks it all in—eyes wide in awe. Suddenly, she releases a smile that brightens the entire room and my heart. This is the Kaniya I have been searching for. A carefree, confident, ambitious young lady who knows that God has a plan to give her hope and a future. We continue to talk for a few more minutes, and then she decides to go back to her room. I continue to sit at the table and watch her as she ascends the stairs and praise God, Jehovah Jireh, for providing tangible evidence that Kaniya and I are both making a breakthrough.

It is the end of the day, and I am preparing to end my fast. I make my way to my secret place to spend some time with the Lord. There is such strength gained while fasting. I now feel stronger and so bold in the assurance of God's power. I hear Him clearly in regard to the matters of His heart and the direction He would have me take. The access that He grants me gives me a deeper connection to Him and allows me to witness another level of His glory. Again, I am so honored and grateful that I am invited to sit at His table and partake of His bread. The Lord instructs me to set the atmosphere by playing the song "Shout to the Lord" by Darlene Zschech. As the words begin to minister to my spirit, I feel its powerful impact just as prominent as I did when I first heard it in 2004 while pregnant with Kaniya. Bathing in the lyrics, I hear God say, "Fast, pray, and move out of My way!" Then suddenly, I see this amazing vision. It is as vivid as a high-definition movie on a twenty-foot outdoor movie screen. I see the parting of the Red Sea. The waves are so high that I cannot tell where the water ends and the sky begins. As I look at the water, I see different types of sea creatures gliding through the water as if they are unbothered. I am standing at the brink of the clear path, and I suddenly look back. There, Kaniya stands—

looking frightened and uncertain. I take her by the hand and assure her that God Almighty is with her. If He is for us, who can be against us (Romans 8:31)? Walking hand in hand, Kaniya and I walk through the Red Sea to the Promised Land. The promise of life, freedom, and prosperity. To see the hands of God move is truly a vision to behold!

It is now around 5:30 p.m., and I am preparing to settle early tonight because today's events have drained me. I begin listening to the song "Atmosphere Shift" by Phil Thompson. I love listening to music containing powerful words that possess the ability to renew my mind and steer me towards the things of God. I am standing in the middle of the living room, and I hear the words of God. He says, "You are a warrior who literally goes in and snatches souls from the pits of hell." I accept this mantle with pride and make the promise to my Father that I will carry out this responsibility until the day that I meet Him in eternity. A little while later, Kaniya enters my room to bid me a good night. We speak very briefly—nothing serious or in great depth. Just small talk and appreciating each other's company. She gives me a status report of what the younger ones are doing upstairs and lets me know that she will be crashing a bit earlier as well. As I prepare to lie down, Kaniya says, "Goodnight,

Mom; tomorrow will be a brand-new day!" I smile in return and say, "Yes, it will." I wonder if Kaniya is aware of how prophetic she really is or how much weight her words carry. I am so stoked to witness what tomorrow holds in regard to the movement of Christ Jesus and the pouring of His oil—His glory!

CHAPTER SEVEN

31 MAY 2020

As I am shaken out of my sleep by the movement and voice of Kaydence, I roll over to find that it is around 3:10 a.m. I am suddenly alarmed because my phone is off due to no power. As I get myself together, I am certain that I have missed my 3:00 a.m. prayer time. My concerns are quickly laid to rest because the hour has just begun—thank God for Kaydence! Kaydence looks at me with this wide-eyed stare, giving me a clear indication that she is not going to sleep anytime soon. Why is she awake? I have no idea, so, at this very moment, I make the decision to conduct prayer and worship in bed. As I begin to pray, the Holy Spirit whispers the song "Passover (Tafi)" by Tomi Favored and Ty Bello in my ear. I hear the crisp melody of her voice constantly repeat "Passover" as the tranquil tune of the piano plays so elegantly in the background. I begin to praise and worship God, and as I do so, I lift every soul residing in my home to Jesus Christ by name: Kelvin Levon, Kaniya, Kelvin Leon, Kendon Levon, Kaydence, and Destiny. I am overcome by the power of God, and I declare and decree the blood of Jesus over their lives—for no evil shall befall them, neither shall any plague come nigh their dwelling (Psalm 91). As I lift them up to heaven, I feel the presence of God. The heaviness of His glory has me pinned to the bed, in which my movement is instantly limited. See, during this hour, the limited movement causes me to evaluate the issues in my heart. God now has permission to address matters that are either masked or unnoticed. In His unveiling, a flash of the strongholds, soul ties, and assignments of the enemy is shown to me. In battle mode, I begin to speak in tongues, binding all works of Satan and loosening them back to the abyss where they belong. Now, I begin to speak life over every person in my family to include myself with the fruit of the Holy Spirit: love, joy, peace, longsuffering, kindness, goodness, faithfulness, gentleness, and self-control (Galatians 5:22–23). For a brief second, I feel the glory of the Lord lift off me. Then suddenly, His glory falls upon me again like the morning's dew! As I continue to praise and worship Him, He begins to download specific instructions of what I am to do on this specific Sunday—the celebration of the day of Pentecost. The Holy Spirit gives me the instructions to, first, walk through and cover the entire house in my heavenly language and anoint each door entrance with blessed oil. Second, wash down all the walls in the house with bleached water while pleading the blood of Jesus during the entire process. Third, conduct noon prayer with the women of God. Fourth, join the entire family together at the beginning of the evening to partake in cooperative prayer. And lastly, bring Kaniya into my prayer room and pray with her so that we can break covenant with all the evil spirits I have subjected her to in the womb. After receiving the instructions, the song "Passover" rings loudly in my ears. I begin to sing the song out loud, allowing the words to saturate my spirit, body, and soul. At this moment, I feel the weight of the Lord fall heavily upon me for the third time! It is different this time, though, because as I am pressed into the bed, I notice that Kaydence has awakened and is trying to sit up. The glory of the Lord is so evident that she cannot move either! She does not panic because the peace of the Lord comforts her. She lies very still and also experiences the mighty glory of the Lord as her cup runneth over (Psalm 23). These magnificent events transpire before the break

The Passover

of dawn. I am assured that what we have experienced in this hour with God Almighty is just the beginning of His powerful encounter.

Around 7:00 a.m. I turn on my war anthem, "Passover." I am in combat mode—ready to destroy anything Satan has in my wake. As the words of the song penetrate my soul like ammunition, I begin to plead the blood of Jesus. I begin to shout "Passover" with power, confidence, and determination. I declare and decree that Satan is not welcomed in my home. I begin to speak in my spiritual language, for it is the secret weapon that explodes on impact and destroys everything that is not of God. I begin to cast down the plots and acts of the enemy by the authority of Jesus Christ. In this instance, the Lord shows me the vision of an army dressed in purple, standing in a formation, and marching into battle. I cannot recognize anyone because the soldiers' faces are covered in war paint. Then, as I squint and stare more intensively at the group, I notice that one of the soldiers' faces is beginning to become exposed. As the image of the soldier's face becomes clearer, I realize that one of the soldiers going into battle is Kaniya! She stands tall with her shoulders back and wears this serious look on her face indicating that she understands that now is the point of no return. She possesses the game face of courage because fear is not her portion, and she wears the whole armor of God. She stands with her loins girt about with truth; her chest is covered with the breastplate of righteousness; her feet are covered with the preparation of the gospel of peace; she holds before her the shield of faith, wearing the helmet of salvation, and carrying the sword of the Spirit (the Word of God) in her right hand (Ephesians 6:13–17). She is now ready for battle—ready to stand against the wiles of Satan and defeat him with the power of Jesus Christ. Jehovah Nissi is her God; therefore, she reigns in victory. Wave white banner, wave!

It is around 8:00 a.m. The Book of Exodus Chapter 12, verse 23, is in full effect. I now sit in my quiet place in worship and prayer, awaiting specific instruction from the Holy Spirit. As I sit in God's presence, the Holy Spirit notifies me that it is time to cover the entire house. Fired up and ready to take action like a well-trained sniper, I begin to walk slowly through the house. As the Holy Spirit highlights the areas that require my attention, I swiftly move my eyes and head from side to side, targeting the object in my line of sight. The scripture Exodus 12:7 is my focal point. I plead the blood of Jesus Christ on every side and top of the doorframes and windows of the entire house. The song "What a Beautiful and Spontaneous Worship" by Amanda Cook and Jeremy Riddle plays softly in the background. Suddenly, the words fill my ears like a rushing wave, and the presence of God hovers over the ceiling, saturates the walls, and covers the floors. I am pressed by the Holy Spirit to go to Kaniya's room, so I beeline upstairs. As I enter her room, I notice that the atmosphere is lighter. Usually, there is a presence so heavy and gloomy here that I am unable to breathe. Not today! I begin to circle the room to cover every corner, every window, every crevice of her space. My presence startles Kaniya as she lifts her head to see who is in her room. She recognizes that it is me, eyeing the small bottle of oil in my hand. She releases a small, innocent smile, and I wink at her to let her know that all is well. She quietly lies her head down on the pillow with utter peace. At this point, God reveals that the distance between Himself and His daughter is no more—heaven and earth have been united once again. Hallelujah, all praises to the King!

It is now 9:30 a.m. I feel as if time is moving at a rapid pace. The Holy Spirit reminds me that *sudden* things are transpiring, and when the hand of God moves, time is not a factor. I acknowledge the wisdom given unto me, and I begin to prepare the atmosphere for praise and worship. I refer to my music library on YouTube.

Scanning the numerous selections, I am compelled to listen to Isi Igenegba as she speaks about God revealing who He is, "Exhortation." As I listen to her teaching that is so elegantly conveyed, God reaffirms that victory is mine! I am so amped up at this moment. I can literally feel the fire of God rushing through my body. The teaching ends, and the song "We Gon' Be Alright" by Tye Tribbett begins to play! I absorb the intense rhythm of the beat, which moves me to bob my head up and down. I take this moment in like a long-lost child and let the words of God penetrate my entire soul. I am so fired up that I do not realize that I am in another part of the house! The song comes to a close, and then I am welcomed by another war anthem. The song "In Jesus' Name" by Tasha Cobbs blasts in the background. In this moment of praise, the Holy Spirit reiterates that I have been conditioned and given the authority to snatch souls from the grips of hell! Pounding my fist in the air and waiving the banner of victory, I sing and shout the lyrics at the top of my lungs. I repeat this affirmation over and over, warning the enemy that we (the Father, Son, Holy Spirit, and I) have arrived on the battlefield. I come in the name of the *Lord*!

10:30 a.m. has swiftly blown in. I have received the second order from the Holy Spirit to wash down the walls

The Passover

of the entire house. I go into the laundry room and begin filling the cleaning bucket with hot water, bleach, and dish detergent. I then begin listening to the song "Take Over" by Theophilus Sunday and allow the Holy Spirit to minister to my soul. Taking my position in the living room, I slowly place my hand into the bucket to grab the washcloth. As if I were performing surgery, I delicately extract a small amount of water from the washcloth and begin washing the walls in a circular motion. After washing the fourth wall, I release this child-like chuckle and ask the Lord, "Why am I washing the walls?" On cue, the Holy Spirit responds, "Like your physical house (made of wood and bricks), your spiritual house (the body) has spots, dirt, residue, and remnants still remaining on the walls. By washing the walls of your physical house, I am allowing you to see in the natural what your spiritual house looks like. Your spiritual house (your temple) is massive. Therefore, some areas that are covered in spots cannot be seen unless you are deliberate in searching for them. As you are cleaning your physical walls, I am simultaneously cleaning your spiritual walls." Suddenly, I began to feel a drunken sensation. I double-check the bucket of water to ensure that it is not the combination of chemicals causing this sensation. No! In fact, it is the presence of the Lord. Yet again, He is blessing me with

His holy presence. Bathed in humility and gratefulness, I make a sincere confession, "Lord, take over my life. I am tired of me!" I can feel His arms around me, giving me this bear hug that allows me to totally surrender. Here I am. Resting soundly in His glory—in His peace.

It is 12:00 p.m. This is the final day of cooperative prayer. Today is the day in which everything God wants to put in me is completely fulfilled in its entirety. I am filled with the confidence that He has come upon me now. I am His complete harvest. This revelation shows me that this entire experience has been about me the whole time! Wow, I hear my Father say, "Well done!" He is well pleased. In the midst of prayer, there is a lot of prophecy being revealed to the women of God (WOG). All eight of us have received a word from the Lord and are given instructions to release it in the group. The words released are so profound and are given as such:

Me: "We are conditioned and ready. Go now!"

WOG 2: "This is all His doing."

WOG 3: "The Holy Spirit is raining on us."

WOG 4: "The gifts are within us. He will make room for us."

The Passover

WOG 5: "His promise. We are ready."

WOG 6: "Our impurities have been burnt out."

WOG 7: "Stay in position. Expect it all to come together when least expected."

WOG 8: "Everything we need, we are filled with it now. Pentecost started seven days ago. Happy birthday to us!"

As all parts of God's Word are joined together, we receive His full revelation:

"Prepare ye the way of the *Lord*. He has conditioned us; we are ready! Go now! He will make room for the gift within us. This is all His doing. He promises that we are ready. Our impurities have been burnt out. We must stay in position and expect it all to come together when we least expect it. Everything we need, we are filled with it now!"

This empowering revelation shakes the very core of the entire group. We are filled with the Spirit of the Lord as His refining fire renews our souls. This day is one I will never forget, for the presence of God is truly amongst us all. I magnify and exalt You, El Shaddai!

It is in the middle of the evening—around 6:30 p.m., to be accurate. I am moving in awe of what Father unveiled to us in the previous hours. I am so moved by His presence that I am unable to remain still, yet a sense of calmness or, perhaps, peace is my gift of the day. I sit on my bed, and I hear a *ding* sound on my cell phone. It is a Facebook alert that Bishop Locklear, a mighty man of God, is on a live recording! I tune in on his live and find that he is teaching about the day of Pentecost. Intrigued, I sit up a bit straighter so that I can give my undivided attention to God's Word. In this teaching, Bishop Locklear references scriptures Mark 16–17, Ezekiel 26:6, Acts 2, and Acts 10:45. He goes on to explain the importance of dreams and their correlation to the unfinished business of God. He makes note that in dreams, God is unveiling (revealing) something to you as you sleep. In this instance, my mind goes to Kaniya—a dreamer whose images are so lucid, so vivid; she often feels as if it is hard to come out of them. I take this gem and store it in my jewelry box so that I am able to give it to Kaniya later today. I tune back into what the bishop is conveying and find that he is now discussing the term *Yada* and the significance of its meaning. He explains that *Yada* means to "perceive, understand and to know [be aware] that Jesus [the Holy Spirit] is in the midst, and the signs will be revealed in their appointed time." He then explains that when the glory of the Lord falls upon us, we will be able to cast out demons in the name of Jesus; we shall speak with new tongues, and the Holy Spirit (Jesus) shall live inside of us—gifting us with a new heart and spirit. This teaching hits me differently today because of what I have witnessed God doing in the past seven days. Now, I have a deeper appreciation of the Pentecost, in which the Lord, our God, came from heaven like a rushing wind and poured His Holy Spirit into man, causing them to speak in fiery tongues (Acts 2:1–4). I acknowledge that it is not by His might or His power but His Spirit that I am whole; I am alive! What I mean about being alive is that my dry bones (my once corpse spirit) are now saturated by the everlasting, sanctified, living water of Jesus Christ. This divine entity has thrust me into greater heights and deeper depths of the heart of my Father. The anointing on my life is not to be handled casually, nor is it to be wasted. My time here is numbered, and there is so much work to be done for the kingdom. The key I hold gives me access to the Holy of Holies—the inner chamber of God's sanctuary, and I will guard it with my life! I boldly make this pledge today with my whole heart, mind, and spirit. May the Lord forever guide me and keep me. Amen.

The day is coming to an end. I feel so empowered, so full of life, and so peaceful in this precious hour. As I move around the kitchen in search of cooking utensils to finish dinner, the songs "Let the Church Say Amen" by Marvin Winans, "I Give Myself Away" by William Mcdowell, and "Worth" by Anthony Brown bless me. The playing of these songs, in this very hour, affirms the covenant made between God and me. In this hour, I can literally feel the hovering of my Father's Spirit over the entire house, and I know without a shadow of a doubt that all is well in the present and future. Very gently, the Holy Spirit tells me that it is time to pray with the entire family. I take a deep breath and begin to muster the formation, for time is of the essence. Kelvin still has not made it home yet, so the children and I are waiting for his arrival. Looking at them, I notice that all four of my irreplaceable gifts are all destined for greatness. They all possess this light that is powerful and captivating—the very attribute of God that will be used in this dark world. I smile, knowing that I am truly a blessed woman. There is a light rattling of keys at the door, and in that brief moment, Kelvin steps in to find us all standing in the dining area. I release a slight smile, greet him, then inform him that dinner is ready. The children eagerly move into the kitchen as if they have not eaten all day.

The Passover

I prepare the younger children and Kelvin's plate, then allow Kaniya and my niece, Destiny, to prepare their plates. After the entire family is settled, I then prepare my plate and head for the table. As I sit down, the kids thank me for the food. They do this at every meal, and it never gets stale. Their warm gesture of appreciation for my labor is greatly appreciated, and my heart beats double time each time they sow this seed of thanks. As everyone begins to eat, I sit very proudly at the opposite head of the table. I take in a deep breath and calmly speak to the entire family about the issues of today's society. I begin to thoroughly explain the uprise of racial brutality and the recent deaths of Black boys and men throughout the country. I encourage them all to be safe, and I then reassure them that the Lord, our God, covers them in accordance with Psalm 91. They all are very attentive, and I can see that they have received my words of encouragement with open arms. As we move on from this heavy topic, I ask them, "Do you all know what this upcoming Sunday will celebrate—the day of Pentecost?" All children, including Destiny, look a bit perplexed, which gives me the indication that they are unaware. I release another slight smile and begin to give a simple yet decent explanation of the day of Pentecost and its significance of why we, as Christians (believers of Jesus, the Christ), celebrate it every year. Again, the children are in a receptive mode, and I quickly realize that Kelvin and I must be more intentional about reading the Bible together as a family to ensure that we are in tune with the knowledge and teaching of Jesus—the foundation of life. Thirty minutes later, this much-needed Bible study is complete, and now it is time to end the night in prayer. I direct everyone to join hands, and I inform Kelvin that I will begin prayer, and he will finish it. He nods in agreement, and we all join hands, creating a circular formation. With heads bowed, all hearts and minds clear, we begin to pray. As I acknowledge our Heavenly Father inwardly, I ask the Holy Spirit to guide me in prayer because He knows the heart of every person in the room and knows what is needed in this time of prayer. As I ask, the Holy Spirit instantly delivers and gives me the words of my Father's heart. I can feel the presence of Christ Jesus in our circle, and it is an indescribable sense of peace. As I finish my portion of prayer, Kelvin immediately picks up without hesitation. His words are so strong, so electric, so piercing. I cannot help but smile because the Spirit of the Lord truly resides in my helpmate. This prayer time is so uplifting. The kids are engaging; they are focused; they are worshiping the Lord by saying amen. Wow! This experience is truly a sight to witness, and I am so honored to be in the midst. At the conclusion of prayer, God graces us all with power, love, and a sound mind. I grab my oil and begin to bless each person in the room by placing a cross on their forehead. The lightness in the room is noticed by us all, and I truly receive in my spirit that we all have accepted what God has set for us to have at this moment: love, peace, joy, and wholeness.

It is after 8:00 p.m. The table is cleared, the kitchen is cleaned, and now is the time for me to have evening prayer. I prepare for my quiet time with the Lord and begin heading to the prayer room. In the process of going into the room, the Holy Spirit instructs me to invite Kaniya to pray with me and, during this time, conduct an impartation into her. These instructions give me a refreshing breath of life—for I know that God is about to do something amazing in the presence of us both! Kaniya is sitting in the living room, watching television. I walk behind her and tap her softly on the shoulder. She looks up at me with that cat-like grin, the one she usually gives when she is unsure of what is about to come her way. I smile and say, "Come on, I invite you to partake in prayer with me tonight." She looks at me with nervous eyes and slowly lets out an "okay." She gently glides from the couch and follows me into my prayer room.

Kaniya has never been in my prayer room before. It is a small, secluded corner in my closet that is elegantly decorated in various shades of purple, gold, cream, and black. The walls are covered with various scriptures, which the Lord gives me to reflect on daily, as well as inspirational décor throughout the area. The soft, LED lighting gives the area a cozy and inviting atmosphere, which makes you feel as if you are in a safe haven. Here is where the presence of the Lord communes with me daily. Kaniya carefully examines my safe space (because she has never been in here before) and then looks at me for further guidance. I can tell that she is nervous, so I assure her that all is well. The presence of the Lord is here, and nothing but goodness dwells in this room. She lets out a light breath and nods, giving me the indication that it is okay to move forward. I take her cue and begin explaining to her the reasoning for her being with me, in this room, at this very hour. I give her the full description of the vision God gave me regarding the condition of her soul. I let her know that I am aware of the darkness that plagues her, the evil spirits that torment her, and the loneliness she feels every day. Her eyes well up with tears, and they immediately fall like raindrops. I grab her hands and let her know that today is the day that she has been pulled into safety. The Lord, our God, has

The Passover

heard her cry and has come to her rescue. She nods her head as if this is the message that she has been waiting to hear for such a long time. Jesus, I can see the desperation plastered on her face as if it were her skin! I know that now is the time to go before the King, the great Jehovah, and make our petition known. In a calming yet bold voice, I begin to pray. During the prayer, I can literally hear the Holy Spirit guiding me on the words to utter from my mouth. While speaking such powerful words, the Holy Spirit directs me to cast down the evil spirits of depression, suicide, darkness, anxiety, insecurity, low self-esteem, rejection, invalidation, instability, deception, manipulation, desolation, displacement, orphanage, isolation, abandonment, offense, defense, doubt, fear, loneliness, resentment, uncertainty, and turmoil. He then instructs me to call forth the divine spirits of love, joy, peace, patience, kindness, goodness, faithfulness, gentleness, self-control, life, acceptance, assurance, stability, and truth. As I speak life over Kaniya, the presence of the Lord hovers over us like a gigantic eagle whose wings engulf us into a cocoon. The love and power of the Lord are truly here—for her gentle squeezing of my hand, the soft swaying of her body, and the total submission of her heart confirm that Kaniya has received *all* that has been sown into her on this day. The glory of the Lord begins to let up, giving me the green light to end the prayer. I end the prayer in Jesus' name and release a heavy sigh that has been sitting on my chest for a very long time. It is such comfort in knowing that the heaviness of our burdens has now been laid at the feet of the altar, and our Father in heaven has dealt with it accordingly. I raise my head and lift Kaniya's head so that she can look me straight in the eyes. She gives me this intense yet subtle stare that compels me to apologize to her for all my shortcomings as a mother and ask for her forgiveness. I am also compelled to encourage her to follow Christ Jesus from this day forth because He will never lead her astray. Kaniya begins to cry again, but this time it is different. It is a cry of hope and joy—one that warms my spirit, body, and soul. Kaniya hugs me very tightly and thanks me for inviting her into prayer. As we exit the prayer room, I realize that this was all part of God's plan and must have taken place for the continual deliverance and healing of us both. Glory to the King of kings and Lord of lords!

Looking back at the past seven days, I acknowledge that our Lord, Jesus Christ, is always present and forever faithful. He shows Himself time and time again, bringing forth the assurance that He is the way and the truth and the life (John 14:6). He loves my daughter and me so

The Passover

much that He allowed me to enter His secret place, in which He gave me insight into the condition of my daughter's soul. He provided me with all I needed to fight this spiritual war, and it is only by His grace that both Kaniya and I are delivered and made whole. Our God has shown me that He is the only true and living God, and besides Him, there is no other. He has revealed to me that the many mantles assigned to Kaniya and me require an anointing that can only be produced by constant pressing and shaking. This oil is invaluable and must be guarded with the utmost care. Looking back over my firstborn's life (even during her time in the womb), I see that Kaniya is destined for greatness; and in that, she will transform this world! The enemy knows this, too; therefore, he will use every scheme possible to try to take her down. However, because she is *chosen*, the mighty God, Jehovah Gibbor, goes before her everywhere her feet tread, and the host of angels assigned over her will always protect her. This champion has many battles to face during her lifetime, but one thing is for certain and another for sure, she will always prevail—she will always *win*! For surely, goodness and mercy shall follow her all the days of her life, and she will dwell in the house of the Lord forever (Psalm 23). *Amen.*

CPSIA information can be obtained
at www.ICGtesting.com
Printed in the USA
BVHW051944270423
663173BV00003B/5